INTRODUCTION TO
SHORTHAND SPEED

INTRODUCTION TO
SHORTHAND SPEED

G. Snodgrass, P.C.T., M.A.C.E.

Head Teacher of Commercial Subjects
Canberra Technical College

Pitman Publishing

First published 1970
Reprinted 1972, 1973

COPYRIGHT

SIR ISAAC PITMAN AND SONS LTD.
Pitman House, Parker Street, Kingsway, London WC2B 5PB
P.O. Box 46038, Portal Street, Nairobi, Kenya

SIR ISAAC PITMAN (AUST.) PTY. LTD.
Pitman House, 158 Bouverie Street, Carlton, Victoria 3053, Australia

PITMAN PUBLISHING COMPANY S.A. LTD.
P.O. Box 11231, Johannesburg, South Africa

PITMAN PUBLISHING CORPORATION
6 East 43rd Street, New York, N.Y. 10017, U.S.A.

SIR ISAAC PITMAN (CANADA) LTD.
495 Wellington Street West, Toronto 135, Canada

THE COPP CLARK PUBLISHING COMPANY
517 Wellington Street West, Toronto 135, Canada

©
Sir Isaac Pitman and Sons Limited
1969

ISBN: 0 273 40096 7

Text set in 8 pt. Monotype Baskerville, printed by photolithography,
and bound in Great Britain at The Pitman Press, Bath
G3—(S.648:24)

Foreword

I recommend this book to students of shorthand whether they are attending a regular class or learning the system within their own home.

Students learning shorthand by correspondence have not had the opportunity to date of progressing beyond mastery of theory, unless assisted by some other person in regular note taking from dictation. The lack of instruction extension to the speed phase of learning has long been deplored. Now by ingenious use in Australasia of mailable discs and correlated shorthand text, Miss G. Snodgrass has come forward with a very timely solution to the problem and I anticipate that it will be received favourably wherever it is used.

A. G. Coxhead
Supervisor of Stenography Courses
New South Wales Department of Technical Education

Preface

THIS book is designed for use by both the class and correspondence student. The correspondence student's efforts will be guided by his correspondence lessons and the class student's by his teacher.

Most of the short forms and important general and special phrases and intersections are covered in lists in this book and some are repeated for extra practice. Several groups of words are also dealt with.

It is suggested to class teachers that one section could be a suitable homework assignment each night. In the lists at the commencement of each page, the longhand could be copied once, short forms ten times, and phrases, intersections and words six times. Copying of outlines aids formation and speed. The lists could be dictated by the teacher next day and checked from the books.

The shorthand pieces should be transcribed *in strict order* (from 1 to 60). Transcription undertaken at home could be corrected in class by the teacher, then dictated to the class at a suitable speed, read by the students, checked from their textbooks, then re-read by the teacher at a rate ten or twenty words a minute higher than previously. The outlines could be re-checked by the students and re-read by the teacher at a rate ten or twenty words a minute higher again. Repetition helps accuracy and speed. In this way, no precious dictation time is lost by a dictation-speed class and each student does a certain amount of homework nightly to help maintain familiarity with correct outlines. The shorthand pieces are designed not only to improve the writer's shorthand speed and accuracy but also to increase his or her English vocabulary and transcription ability.

A key to this book is also available.

Introduction

In shorthand, copy dictation is the taking down of matter while copying from shorthand. This dictation may be timed or untimed. Speed work is the taking down of unseen matter at a set rate of reading.

In speed work there is a necessity for instantaneous mental and manual response and co-ordination of the senses is under constant pressure. Automaticity of response results from complete familiarization with the signs and symbols. Thorough memorization not only of the common outlines but also of the short forms and phrases assists this process.

Consistent effort, regular practice and full concentration are needed for the best results in both copy dictation and unseen speed work. As much matter as possible should be written or read back. Repetition of dictation at slightly higher rates helps to improve speed and accuracy.

NOTEBOOKS AND HOW TO USE THEM

A loose-leaf reporter's notebook ensures both a flat surface and the easy removal of any sheets if necessary for transcription.

The students should work through the book one way, then turn the book around and write on the other side of all the sheets. This ensures ease of turning over. Another aid to turning a leaf is the placing of the left thumb behind the left-hand lower corner and gradually easing up the sheet until it can be turned over in a flash at the appropriate moment. (The opposite would apply to left-handed people.)

Draw a line one inch down from the left-hand edge of the notebook (left-handed people can draw it on the right). Any special notations can be placed in this margin, and the remaining narrower page ensures a quicker and easier hand movement.

OUTLINES

Be consistent in the size of outlines. Keep ordinary strokes one-sixth of an inch in length, half-length strokes one-twelfth of an inch and double-length strokes one-third of an inch. Do not leave unnecessary spaces between outlines, and write from the margin to the extreme right-hand edge of the page.

Use a fine, flexible pen (either dip nib in the early stages or special fountain pen) to aid formation and to allow good distinction between light and heavy strokes. Never use a pencil.

It should not be necessary to insert many vowels in ordinary matter, other than the insertion of the dot *i* in *him, himself* or *position* in phrases, and a vowel in any words the writer feels need vocalization. Proper names or unusual matter should have as much vocalization as possible. It is also wise to insert as many diphthongs as possible as words containing these are often more difficult to transcribe. Many vowels are given in this book as an aid to transcription. On the whole these need not be shown in dictation.

Full stops and capital letters must be indicated. It is permissible to join the bottom of the full stop for quickness in speed, e.g., ..𝑥.... (commence from the left). Two small strokes indicating a capital should be written forwards and upwards in readiness for writing the next word.

Where attention needs to be drawn to one or two words only (or one or two words are quoted), it is quicker to underline the outline or outlines with a wavy line rather than use inverted commas.

FALLING BEHIND THE READER

Do not panic if you fall behind the reader. A phrase will often permit you to catch up. If it is necessary to omit a word or words, leave a space and then continue with as much of the piece as possible. It is often wise to be one or two words behind the reader as this can aid phrasing and correct outline formation. Do not waste time over a difficult outline.

LONGHAND IN NOTE TAKING

Longhand should not appear in the shorthand notes, with these exceptions:

1. Initials (and usually separate letters, other than *a* or *I*).
2. Proper names having unusual spelling.
3. The abbreviation a.m. and similar ones likely to be misread if the shorthand outline is written.
4. The figures 8, 10 and 18. (These could be confused with other outlines.) Numbers from 21 upwards.
5. Mathematical formulae, etc.

1

Copy the following phrases on were, was, would and word

they were
we were

and were
that were

those were
if it were

if there were
for there were

you were
who were

which were
were the

it was
who was

which was
I was

and was the
that was

this was
although there was

it would be
would you

he would not care
which would

you would
I would be

we would
they would

this would do
and would

that would be
my word

their word
our words

in our own words
these words

that this would be the
in other words

satisfactory words
many words

Transcribe the following

Copy the following intersections

county council
local council

suburban council
Australian
  Government

Government of
  Australia
government backing

government policy
party government

political party
right purpose

Northern Territory
Department of the
  Navy

merchandise
  department
sports department

extra charge
free of charge

charge officer
Journal of
  Education

Financial Journal
Captain Brown

your government
capital expenditure

Victorian capital
firm's capital

capital punishment
Farraday Co. Ltd.

wool company
Colonel Edwards

Major Rees
Professor Jones

special attention
Minister for the Army

opposing party
in the early morning

Commonwealth Bank
river bank

parliamentary bill
bill of lading

lucrative business
copper business

Transcribe the following passage

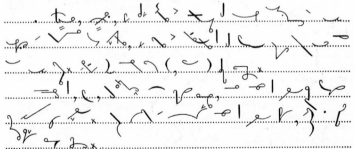

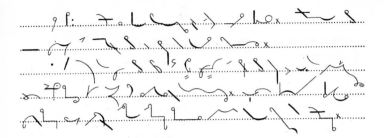

3

Copy the following phrases on doubling

if there/their
in other words ....

back their words
follow their
  instructions ....

we have their
upon their ....

spoke their
making their way....................

I had been there
carried on their ....

I hope there will be
some other means ....

some other directions
or some other ....

my dear friend
my dear madam ....

Copy the following sets of distinctive outlines

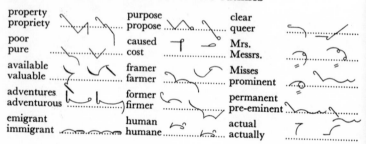

property
propriety ....

poor
pure ....

available
valuable ....

adventures
adventurous ....

emigrant
immigrant ....

purpose
propose ....

caused
cost ....

framer
farmer ....

former
firmer ....

human
humane ....

clear
queer

Mrs.
Messrs.

Misses
prominent

permanent
pre-eminent

actual
actually

Transcribe the following passage

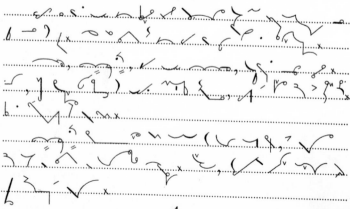

4

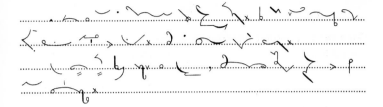

4

Copy the following Countries or States

Great Britain United Kingdom		Northern Territory South Australia	
Australia United States		Western Australia Tasmania	

United States of
    America
New South Wales
		Australian Capital
		    Territory
		New Zealand	

Victoria Queensland		Canada Malaysia	

Copy the following words containing stroke "ing"

having
joining

making
fishing

avoiding
spending

auctioning
travelling

ruining
driving

skating
planning

Transcribe the following passage

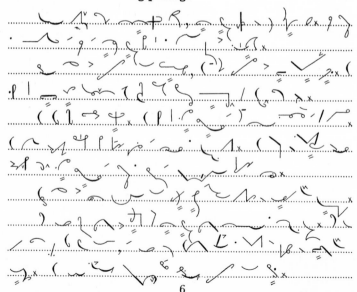

6

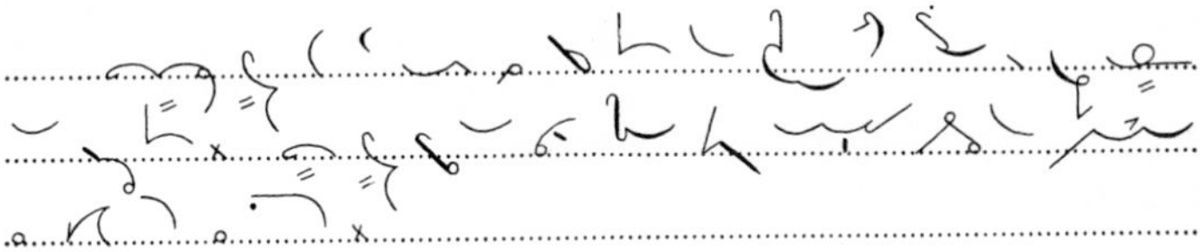

5

Copy the following phrases on hooks

copy of
rate of exchange

side of the
in charge of

which have been
we had been

in our view
in our ways

at all costs
financial position

better than
bigger than

carried on the
in your own opinion

our own minds
which can only do

they will only think
which appears that

he appears to be
who have known

on Saturday evenings
Thursday evening

Wednesday afternoons
yesterday afternoon

political associations
wood association

for your information
at all events

out of doors
into effect

right effect
I had been

Transcribe the following letter

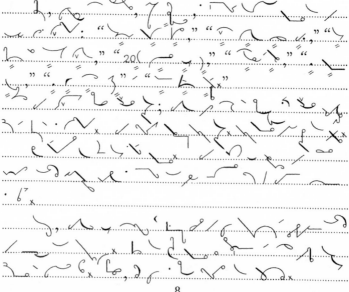

8

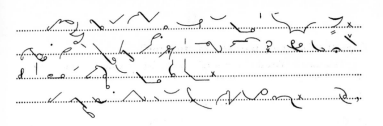

6

Copy the following phrases on "tick the"

1. Downward "tick the" is generally used after straight strokes from left to right and anti-clockwise curves or circles or joined dipththongs

| of the | | that the | |
| to the | | value the | |

| put the | | knows the | |
| by the | | decides the | |

| remember the | | saves the | |
| placing the | | commence the | |

2. Upward "tick the" is generally used after *t* or *d*, straight strokes from right to left or clockwise curves or circles

| at the | | wish the | |
| do the | | may the | |

| which the | | was the | |
| on the | | seems the | |

| charge the | | sells the | |
| shall the | | desires the | |

3. Upward "tick the" is generally used after anti-clockwise hooks and downward "tick the" is generally used after clockwise hooks (this does not apply where it follows a straight horizontal or straight upstroke finally hooked for *n*, when the upward "tick the" is used; e.g., run the ⟋ crown the ⟿.)

| find the | | demand the | |
| mention the | | condone the | |

| have been the | | open the | |
| quality of the | | earn the | |

Transcribe the following passage

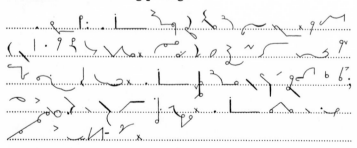

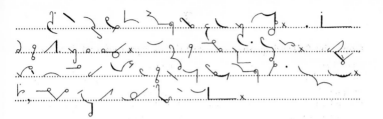

7

Copy the following phrases containing upward and downward l

later than any later than		those letters this letter		
no later than please let us		business letters cross the line		
please let us know let us have the		for these lines of silent		
to let you have longer than		in silent please lend		
no longer than our letters		it is not like the it is like the		

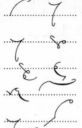
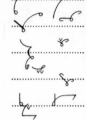

Copy the following list of outlines which sometimes give trouble

	transcribe		solicitor	
start self-starter	transcribe merchandise		solicitor behaviour	
material exactly	warehouse swerved		solitary dwelt	

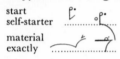

Transcribe the following letter

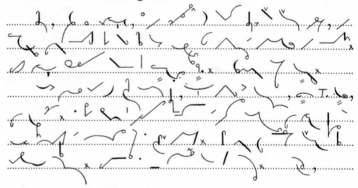

Transcribe the following passage

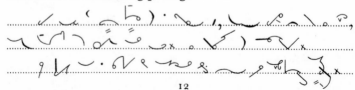

12

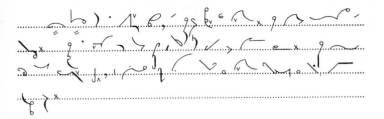

8

Copy the following intersections

at the beginning of the
attractive cover

beginning of the book
necessary form

Federal Ministry
Federal Parliament

valuation of the
property
property valuation

convenient time
at their convenience

month of March
summer months

direct authority
general manager

note: much more

Minister for the Navy
minister of religion

local minister
Minister for Defence

I have mentioned
it was mentioned

national affairs
national radio

heavy industry
local council

in reply to your inquiry
we have made inquiries

communication system
regular communication

Transcribe the following letter

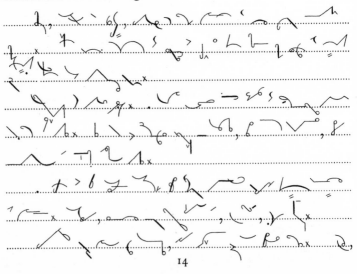

14

Transcribe the following letter

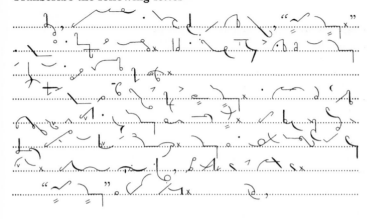

9

Copy the following phrases on halving

if it is to be
in which it may be

they will not be
some time ago

for which it can be
unable to go

you are able to make
I am not

from time to time
for some time past

at the same time
at all times

Copy the following phrases on circles

as is, as his
is as, is his

as we may be able to
as we do the

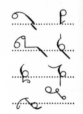

as soon as we can
please let us know

charge us
for us

as we have been
as we think

as well as it can be
on this subject

this statement
in this city

will you please send
as soon as possible

Transcribe the following letter

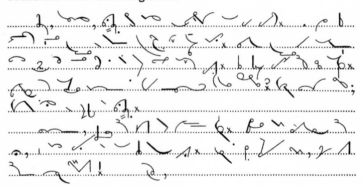

Transcribe the following passage

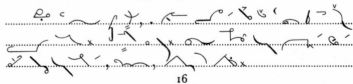

16

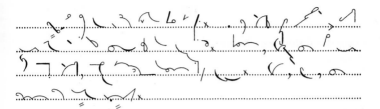

10

Copy the following phrases

$8
$500 ....

5%
2½% per
annum ....

£9,000
£500,000 ....

$7,000
$8.25 ....

5¼% com-
mission
8¾% discount ....

500 lbs
1,000 lbs ....

Copy the following words ending in -ly

deeply
possibly ....

attractively
attentively ....

faintly
poorly ....

beautifully
peacefully ....

friendly
jointly ....

recently
neatly ....

peaceably
delightfully ....

instantly
constantly ....

completely
vividly ....

Transcribe the following passage

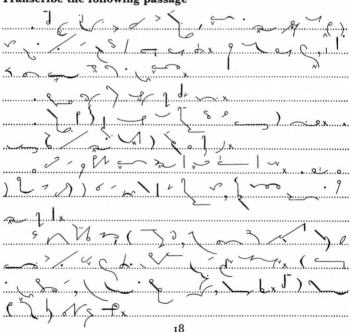

Transcribe the following letter

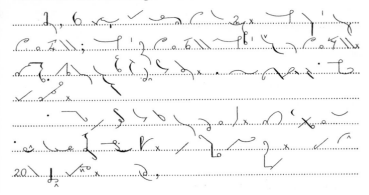

11

Copy the following intersections

we shall require
all your requirements

Society of Musicians
commonwealth railways

Australian community
Australian Government

railway management
necessary arrangements

Commonwealth of
   Australia
conservative policy

please arrange the
   matter
liberal government

this house
Royal Society

Gas Co. Ltd.
Hirst Limited

Copy the following short forms

investigation
itself

largest
largely

northern
November

January
knowledge

liberty
mortgage-d

objection
expenditure

language
larger

neglect-ed
nevertheless

opportunity
organization

Transcribe the following passage

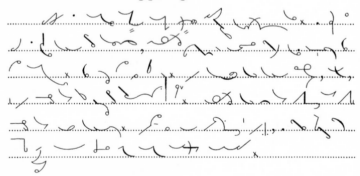

Transcribe the following letter

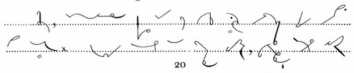

20

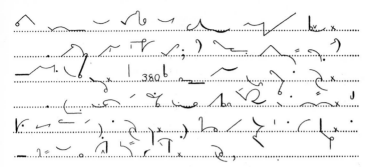

Copy the following phrases on loops

at first cost
in the first instance

October next
in the first place

Wednesday first
Thursday next

first day
first-class

Friday next
February first

first of all
first position

Copy the following short forms

published
rather

shall
short

surprised
telegram

regular
remarkable-ly

significance
significant

tell
thank-ed

represent-ed
respect-ed

signify-ied
something

that
themselves

respectful-ly
responsible-
ility

southern
speak

therefore
third

satisfaction
satisfactorily

special-ly
spirit

organize
probability

school
schooled

subject-ed
sufficient-
ly-cy

owing
owner

sent
several

sure
surprise

publication
pleasure

Transcribe the following letter

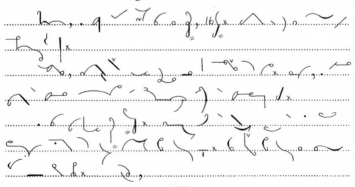

Transcribe the following letter

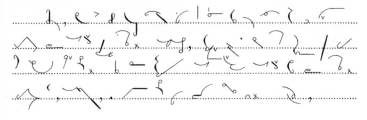

13

Copy the following phrases on omissions

about the matter
as if it were possible

one or two
right or wrong

as early as possible
as quickly as possible

out of place
short space of time

in a position
as we have received

most probably
point of view

no reply
last week

we are glad to know
whether it is possible

miles per hour
business man

it seems to me
north and south

business men
in the circumstances

ways and means
Mr. and Mrs.

Transcribe the following passage

24

Transcribe the following letter

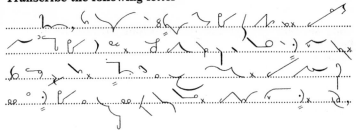

14

Copy the following pairs of distinguishing outlines based on the halving principle

regard		mountain		evidence	
regret		maintain		avoidance	
secret		editor		evidently	
sacred		auditor		eventually	
unavoidable		support		hotly	
inevitable		separate		hotel	
garden		written		evident	
guardian		routine		confident	

Copy the following short forms

general-ly		important-ce		inform-ed	
financial-ly		impossible		information	
gentleman		improve-d-ment		inscribe-d	
gentlemen		income		inscription	
govern-ed		inconvenience-t-ly		instruction	
government		individual-ly		instructive	
they are		inspect		insurance	
this		near		interest	
however		influence		something	
immediate		influenced		special	

Transcribe the following passage

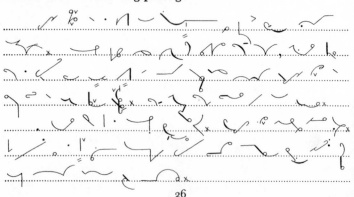

26

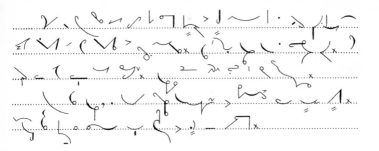

15

Copy the following short forms

those till		United States university		whose wonderful-ly		
toward trade		usual-ly welcome		word writer		
tried truth		whenever whether		yard yesterday		

Copy the following words containing medial semi-circle w

twelfth frequently		bewildered sandwiches		seaworthy fireworks
subsequently farewell		goodwill misquotation		quality somewhat

Transcribe the following passage

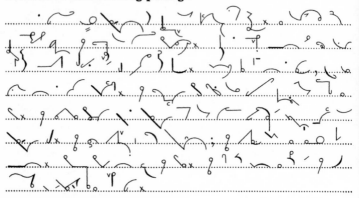

Transcribe the following letter

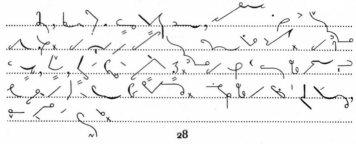

28

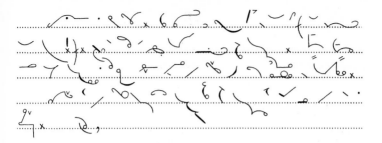

16

Copy the following phrases on omissions

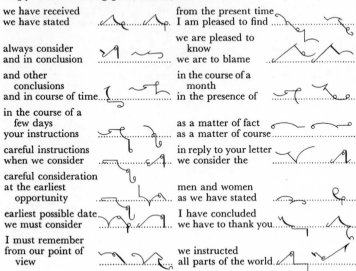

we have received
we have stated

always consider
and in conclusion

and other
  conclusions
and in course of time

in the course of a
  few days
your instructions

careful instructions
when we consider

careful consideration
at the earliest
  opportunity

earliest possible date
we must consider

I must remember
from our point of
  view

from the present time
I am pleased to find

we are pleased to
  know
we are to blame

in the course of a
  month
in the presence of

as a matter of fact
as a matter of course

in reply to your letter
we consider the

men and women
as we have stated

I have concluded
we have to thank you

we instructed
all parts of the world

Transcribe the following passage

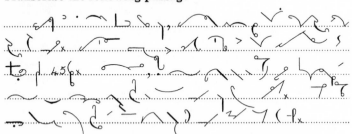

Transcribe the following letter

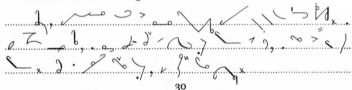

30

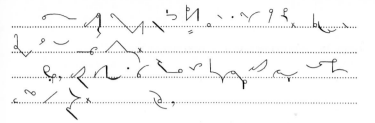

17

Copy the following phrases containing "much"

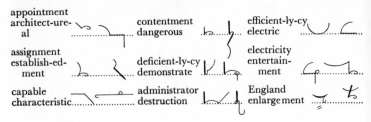

so much
too much

how much
as much as

inasmuch as
as much as
possible

Copy the following short forms

appointment
architect-ure-
al

contentment
dangerous

efficient-ly-cy
electric

assignment
establish-ed-
ment

deficient-ly-cy
demonstrate

electricity
entertain-
ment

capable
characteristic

administrator
destruction

England
enlargement

Transcribe the following passage

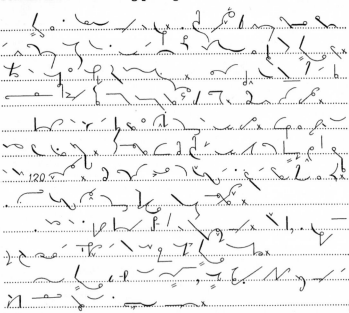

Transcribe the following letter

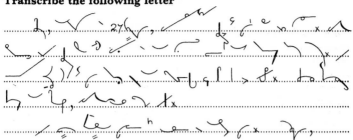

18

Copy the following phrases on omissions

all we possibly can
and instructed

we have instructed
it has occurred to us

point to be taken into
consideration
at the present moment

animal life
balance of the order

between now
between this

kindly consider the
matter
of his having received

your directions
take into consideration
the fact

lowest price
more or less

in relation to
side by side

for the sake of
just possible

worth while
best of our ability

early consideration
from first to last

in consequence of
this class of material

bear in mind
additional expense

early reply
for the first time

end of the month
on the contrary

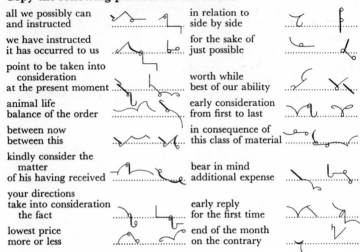

Transcribe the following passage

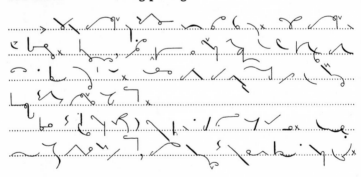

Transcribe the following letter

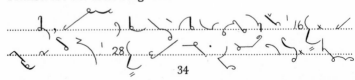

34

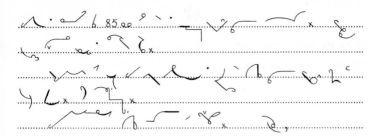

19

Copy the following short forms

enlarge
emergency

wonderful-ly
word

opinion
expensive

enthusiastic
bankruptcy

writer
university

expediency
identical

executive
executor

young
yesterday

identification
imperfect-ion-
ly

Copy the following words on prefixes

circumference
consequent

introduce
magnificently

transacted
translation

accomplished
accommodated

self-denial
self-
confidently

inhabited
instructed

Transcribe the following passage

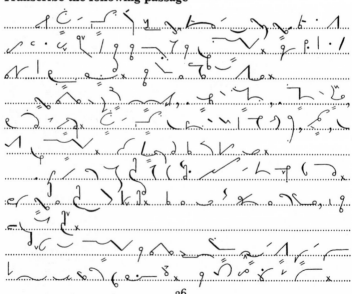

36

Transcribe the following letter

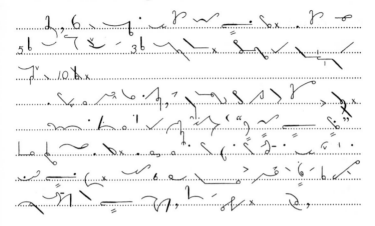

20

Copy the following words containing negative prefixes

unnecessary
unnamed

illogical
illegal

irradiance
irrefutable

unknown
immoderate

illimitable
irreclaimable

irrevocable
irrational

immaterial
illegible

irreducible
irredeemable

irreplaceable
irresistible

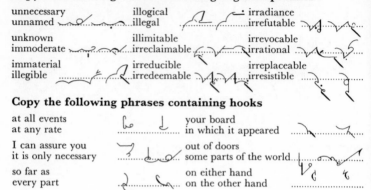

Copy the following phrases containing hooks

at all events
at any rate

your board
in which it appeared

I can assure you
it is only necessary

out of doors
some parts of the world

so far as
every part

on either hand
on the other hand

Transcribe the following passage

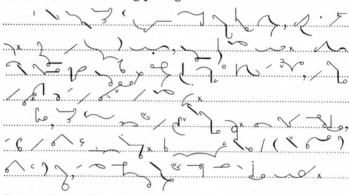

Transcribe the following letter

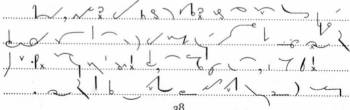

38

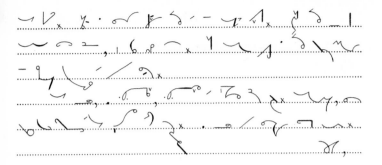

21

Copy the following short forms

incorporated
independent-
ly-ce
indispensable-
ly
influential-ly

introduction
investment
irregular
jurisdiction
justification
legislative

legislature
manufac-
ture-d
manu-
facturer
manuscript
mathe-
matics
maximum

intelligence
intelligent-ly

Copy the following words containing dot "ing"

deserving
coughing
cautioning
rinsing

shining
hearing
spying
repeating

muttering
abiding
thinking
exchanging

Transcribe the following passage

Transcribe the following letter

1,132,608

40

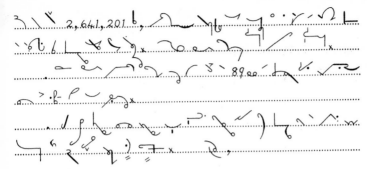

22

Copy the following business phrases

annual general meeting
declare a dividend

yours sincerely
always consider

unless we receive the
order
we hope you will be
able to

in the course of a few
days
as we have had a letter

as soon as we receive
a reply
best trade terms

brought forward
we can quote you

present state of the
market
if possible

registered letter
in the presence of

we are glad to have
the order
in your reply to
my letter

on the one hand
on the other hand

Chairman of
Directors
Board of Directors

ordinary shares
preference shares

postal order
income tax

financial position
by passenger train

Transcribe the following passage

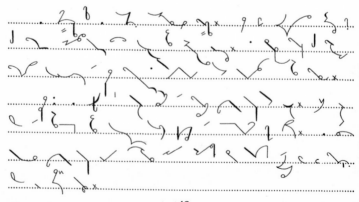

42

Transcribe the following letter

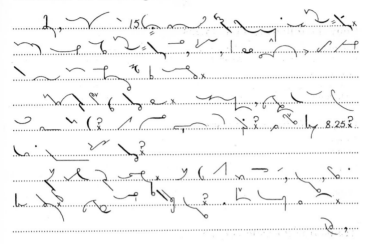

23

Copy the following short forms

minimum
misfortune

objectionable
passenger

performance
practicable

negligence
notwith-
standing

peculiar-ity
perform-ed

preliminary
production

Copy the following phrases

for me
to him

it will be
and will be

for myself
for himself

for which it will be
who will do

in whom
for her

will not be able to
chairman said

Transcribe the following passage

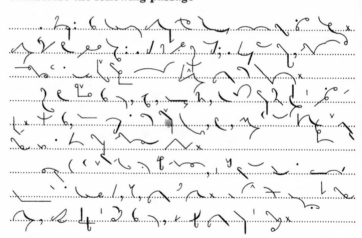

Transcribe the following passage

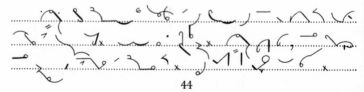

44

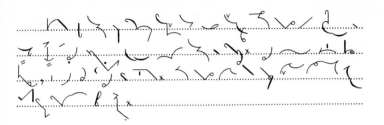

24

Copy the following short forms

accord-ing acknowledge		cannot cared		difficult difficulty
advantage advertise-d-ment		certificate character		distinguished during
altogether anything		cheered child		English equal-ly
balanced become		circumstance cold		especial-ly everything
becoming behalf		commercial-ly danger		exchange-d expect-ed
build-ing called		deliver-y-ed description		familiar February

Copy the following words containing dot hay

uphill
downhill

likelihood
neighbourhood

misapprehension
comprehension

womanhood
household

perhaps
girlhood

armhole
mishear

Copy the following words with con- or com- in full

commotion
commissioner

commerce
commercialize

consul
consular

Copy the following words with -ship in full

fellowship
flagship

steamship
airship

warship
worship

Transcribe the following passage

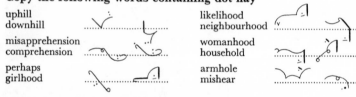
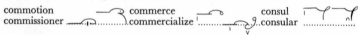

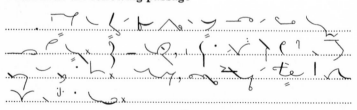

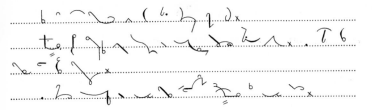

25

Copy the following phrases on doubling

has to be there
has been there

gain their
confidence
my dear friend

for which there is
I think there may
be

my dear madam
some other means

having their way
whenever there is

in some other ways
seek their opinion

spoke their words
knowing their
opinions

reopen their
done their

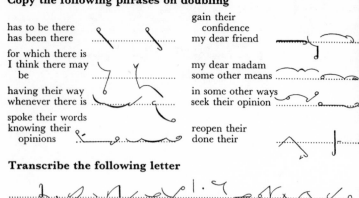

Transcribe the following letter

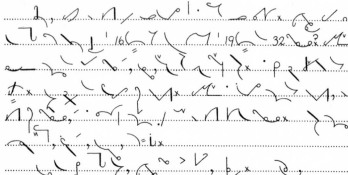

Transcribe the following passage

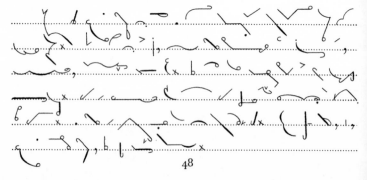

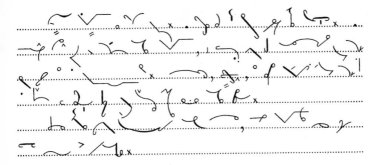

26

Copy the following short forms

productive project-ed		republican respective		sympathetic telegraphic	
proportion-ed prospective		respectively selfish-ness		thankful unanimous-ly	
publisher questionable-ly		sensible-ly-ility stranger		uniform-ity-ly universal-ly	
reform-ed remarkable		subscribe-d subscription		universe valuation	
representation republic		substantial-ly suspect-ed		abandonment administratrix	
reformer advertise-d-ment		discharge-d defective		electrical arbitration	

Transcribe the following letter

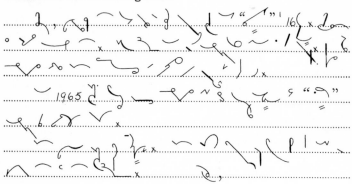

Transcribe the following letter

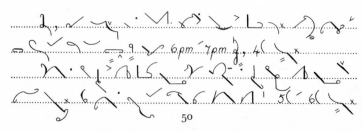

50

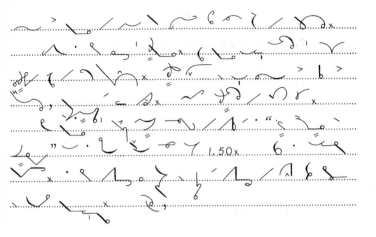

27

Copy the following words containing suffixes

consignment imprisonment		regimental detrimental		citizenship censorship	
effacement deferment		departmentally heedfulness		friendship relationship	
achievement settlement		heedlessness carelessness		salesmanship scholarship	
agreement treatment		carefulness credulousness		psychological pathological	

Transcribe the following passage

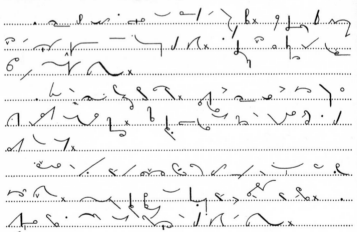

Transcribe the following passage

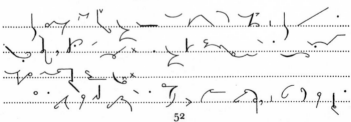

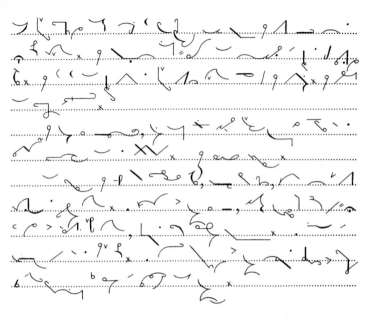

53

28

Copy the following political phrases

Houses of Parliament
Member of Parliament

tax payers
income tax

Governor-General
honourable member

ordinary rates
adjournment of the
House

Prime Minister
Leader of the
Opposition

Liberal Party
Labour Party

honourable senator
in the House of
Representatives

old age pensions
Australian
Commonwealth

Upper House
Lower House

address in reply
party leaders

Federal Government
member of the
opposition

Legislative Assembly
Legislative Council

Copy the following phrases on omissions

fact of the matter
at the moment

in the statement
as near as possible

in our reply
bill of exchange

I have not been able to
not yet received

Transcribe the following passage

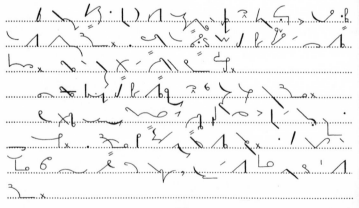

54

Transcribe the following letter

29

Copy the following short forms

certificate		expected		destructive		
character		amalgamate		enlarger		
commercial		amalgamation		enlightenment		
description		arbitrate		executrix		
different		attainment		exigency		
destruction		contingency		extinguish-ed		
		cross-examination				
difficulty		denomina-tional		familiarize		
English				generalization		

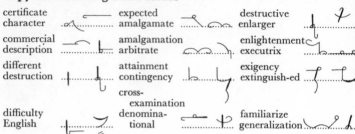

Transcribe the following letter of reference

Transcribe the following letter

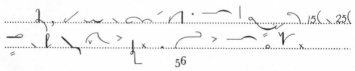

56

30

Copy the following words containing intervening vowels

bold		apartment		furnish	
charm		attorney		furniture	
Charles		before		further	
church		civility		garden	
coarse/course		collect		guardian	
court		college		lecture	
curse		cordial		literature	
curt		corner		normal	
curve		correct		occurred	
dark		correspondent		occurrence	
George		courage		outdoor	
north		courtesy		parallel	
nurse		darling		parcel	
shark		department		purchase	
sharp		direct		record	
Turk		fixture		regard	
accordance		forget		shorter	
accordingly		fulfil		Thursday	

Transcribe the following passage

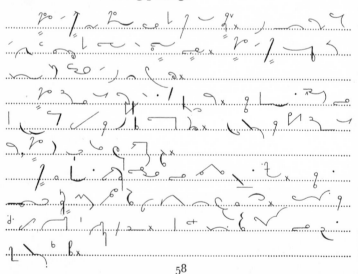

Transcribe the following letter

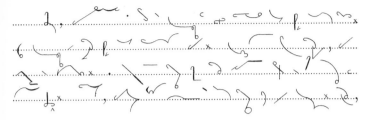

31

Copy the following phrases containing intersections

by return of post
declare a dividend

ex dividend
under separate cover

at your early convenience
capital punishment

captain in the army
form of the report

please mention the facts
my attention has been
called

I have to call attention
present state of the market

fire insurance company
life assurance company

third party insurance
some months ago

Transcribe the following letter

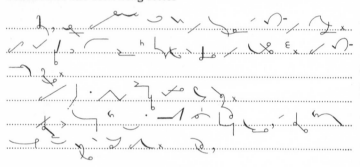

Transcribe the following passage

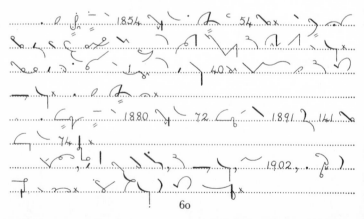

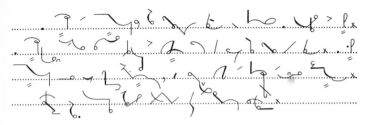

32

Copy the following words containing half-length strokes

exactly
fitly

vividly
completely

boldly
tightened

traded
credited

promptness
tightness

aptness
boldness

mildness
hesitatingly

inert
ultimate

indicate
indicated

undoubted
indebted

undated
remotely

pilot
drunkard

scampered
auctioned

glared
coloured

insulate
heart

Copy the following political phrases

honourable gentleman
Postmaster General

Leader of the House
honourable senator

Federal Executive
Federal Treasurer

next session
this session

Transcribe the following piece

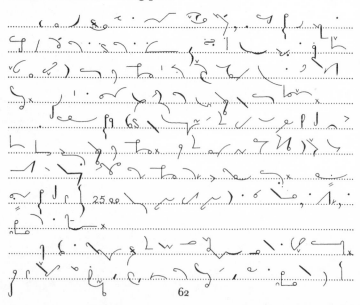

62

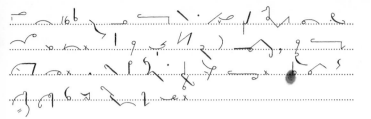

33

Copy the following short forms

familiar-ity
February

financial-ly
general-ly

govern-ed
government

immediate
income

imperturbable
inconsiderate

informer
intelligible-ly

irremovable-ly
irrespective

irresponsible-
ility
magnetic-ism

mathematical-ly
mathematician

metropolitan
obstruction

obstructive
performer

inconvenience
individual-ly

Transcribe the following letter

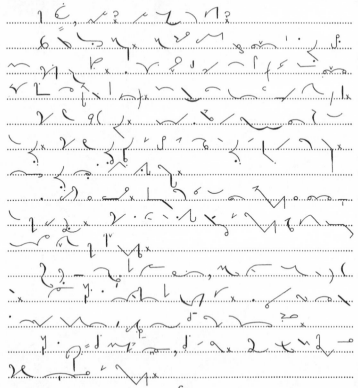

64

Transcribe the following passage

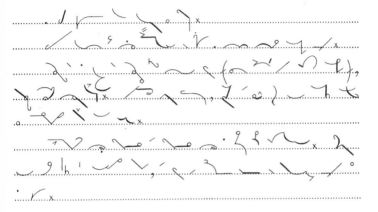

34

Copy the following present and past-tense verbs

wonder		surrender		answer	
wondered		surrendered		answered	
render		slander		defer	
rendered		slandered		deferred	
wander		launder		prefer	
wandered		laundered		preferred	
winter		linger		refer	
wintered		lingered		referred	
hinder		conquer		prepare	
hindered		conquered		prepared	

Transcribe the following passage

Transcribe the following letter

66

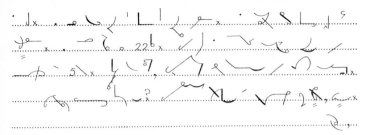

35

Copy the following phrases containing hooks

ought to have known
local associations

medical association
all parts of the globe

in a position
major part

forty parts
their boards

Copy the following words which sometimes give trouble

appreciate
destiny

casualty
assurance

discern
downright

Note: under review

Transcribe the following passage

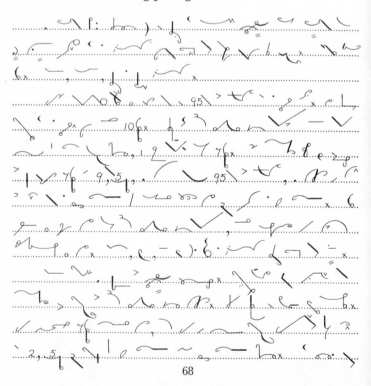

68

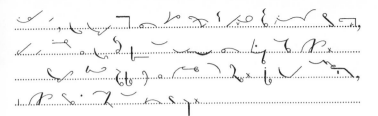

36

Copy the following short forms

influenced inform-ed		itself perspective		removable reproduction	
inscribe-d inscription		proficient-ly-cy knowledge		retrospect retrospection	
inspect-ed-ion interest		prospectus recoverable		subjective signification	
investigation January		demonstration relinquish-ed		satisfactory subjection	

Transcribe the following passage

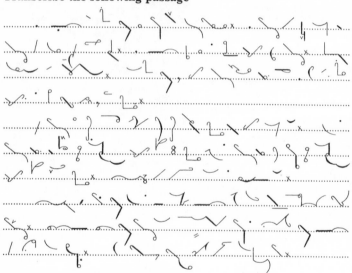

Transcribe the following letter

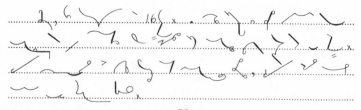

70

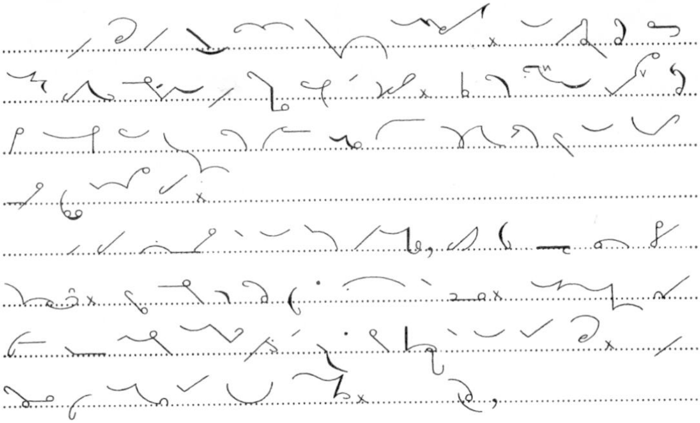

37

Copy the following words ending in -elty, -ility, -rity

utility
dexterity

minority
suitability

adaptability
accessibility

novelty
majority

feasibility
popularity

facility
ability

Note: Australian Capital Territory .... New South Wales ....

Transcribe the following piece

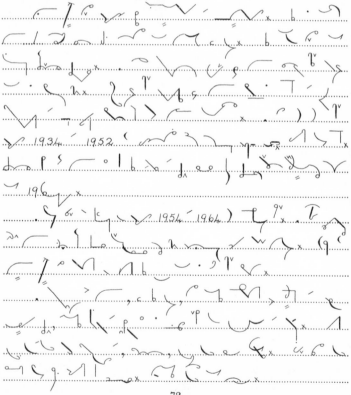

Transcribe the following passage

38

Copy the following phrases

state of affairs
difference of opinion

most probably
telegraph office

shorthand writer
words a minute

industrial life
towards one another

in other respects
technical college

to a great extent
in the first place

Transcribe the following passage

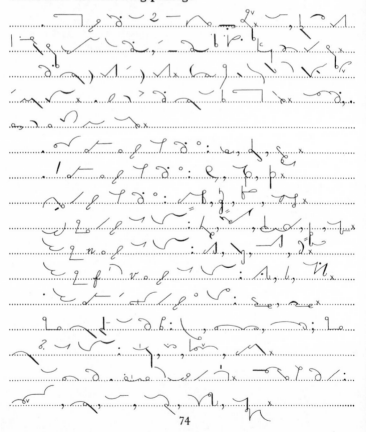

74

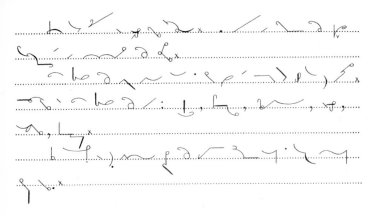

39

Copy the following short forms

largely		nevertheless		universality	
liberty		northern		unprincipled	
mortgage-d		never		wheresoever	
neglect-ed		organization		whithersoever	

Transcribe the following passage

[shorthand outlines]

1788.

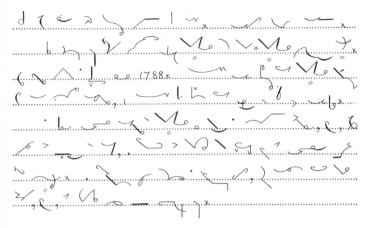

1788

40

Copy the following words with upward "sh"

fish		shaker		shoulder	
dash		sugar		slashed	
Swedish		shimmer		polished	
brush		chauffeur		abolished	
atrocious		shiver		extenuation	
sheaf		shawl		continuation	
shave		shoal		sanctioned	
sheath		sheltered		mentioned	

Copy the following business phrases

by the directors		ex dividend	
of the company		interim dividend	
to the company		bank note	
Stock Exchange		bank rate	
stocks and shares		additional cost	
report and accounts		additional expense	

Transcribe the following

[shorthand outlines — contains dates 1940, 1952, 1961, 58]

41

Copy the following words which sometimes give trouble

illness
allowance

mythology
admiralty

allocation
occurrence

alliance
delightful

publicity
coverage

dazzle
resume

Note: mature maturity

Transcribe the following piece

79

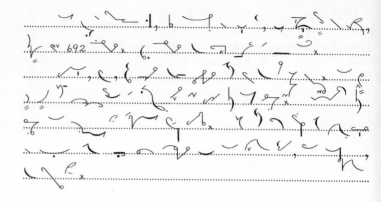

42

Copy the following pairs of distinguishing outlines

gentleman
gentlemen

anybody
nobody

factor
factory

agent
agency

matter
mature

fresh
afresh

personal
personnel

dearest
dressed

mistook
mistake

Copy the following short forms

organize
practice

rather
regular

respectful-ly
responsible-
ility

practise-d
probable-ly-
ility

remarkable
represent-ed

significance
southern

prospect
publication

representative
respect-ed

sufficient-ly-
cy
telegram

assignment
university

contentment
capable

defective
deficient-ly-
cy

enlarge
enlargement

identical
identification

executive
discharge-d

Transcribe the following passage

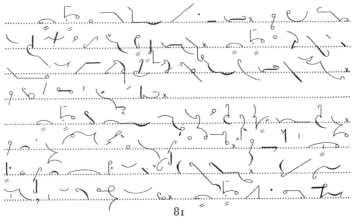

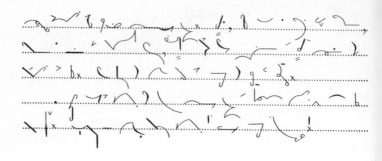

43

Copy the following phrases

expression of opinion
notwithstanding the fact

last month
at your earliest convenience

for their immediate
end of the month

in such a matter
freedom of the press

Transcribe the following letter

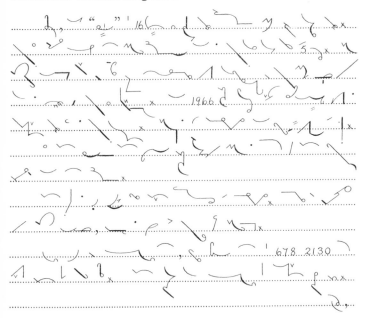

Transcribe the following passage

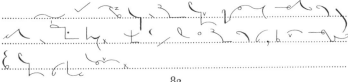

44

Copy the following words containing medial hook n

arrangement
orange

vanish
finish

attended
painted

furnished
furniture

dining
joining

London
appointed

fancy
banish

regaining
lonesome

plenty
planted

Spanish
French

finding
apparently

blended
agent

Copy these words with circles or loops to initial hooks

springs
struggled

switchers
sweeter

stuttering
staggering

straight-
forward
seeker

swaggers
sweepers

stopper
stitcher

Transcribe the following passage

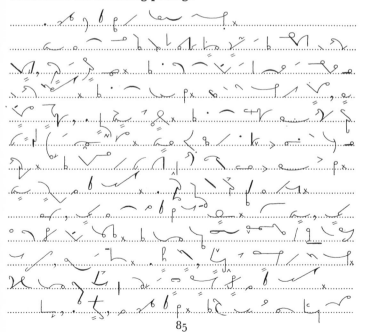

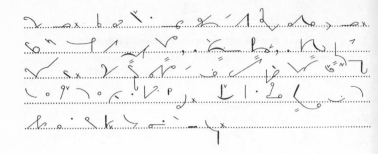

45

Copy the following short forms

therefore		yesterday		characteristic	
together		appointment		dangerous	
welcome		architect-ure-al		demonstrate	
whatever		disrespect		demonstration	

Transcribe the following letter

4—(S.648)

Transcribe the following passage

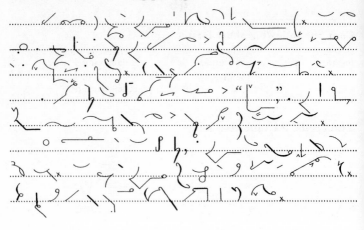

46

Copy the following business phrases

from the last report
in reply to your inquiry

your ability
rest of their ability

letter of credit
best of our ability

workers' compensation
consolidated revenue

from the moment
discount for cash

ordinary rates
general manager

Copy the following legal phrases

articles of association
your honour

his honour
Court of Appeal

High Court of Australia
form of affidavit

deed of settlement
deed of transfer

counsel for the defence
counsel for the prosecution

counsel for the defendant
justice of the peace

Copy the following words used in legal offices

alimony
anomaly

arbitration
attorney

bankruptcy
bequeath

codicil
defendant

devise
equitable

executor
intestate

larceny
mortgage

plaintiff
probate

statutory
subpoena

Transcribe the following passage

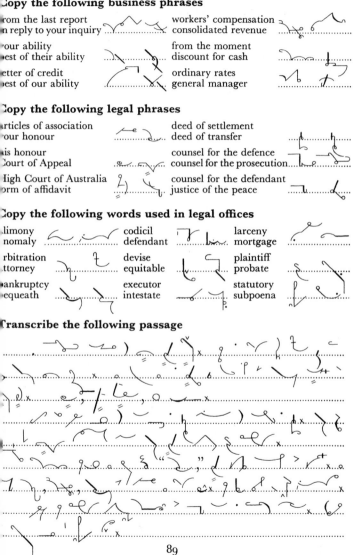

89

47

Copy the following short forms

difficult
efficient-ly-cy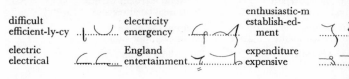

electricity
emergency

enthusiastic-m
establish-ed-
ment

electric
electrical

England
entertainment

expenditure
expensive

Transcribe the following passage

90

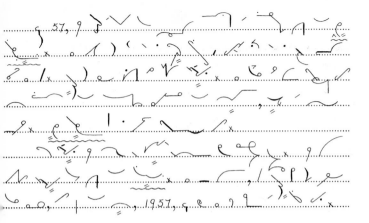

48

Copy the following words containing medial stroke n

bonnet denied	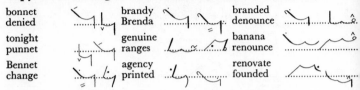	brandy Brenda		branded denounce	
tonight punnet		genuine ranges		banana renounce	
Bennet change		agency printed		renovate founded	

Copy the following words containing downward l

film realm	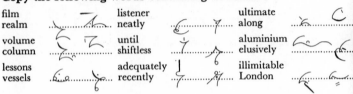	listener neatly		ultimate along	
volume column		until shiftless		aluminium elusively	
lessons vessels		adequately recently		illimitable London	

Transcribe the following passage

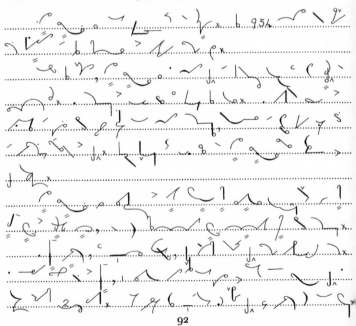

92

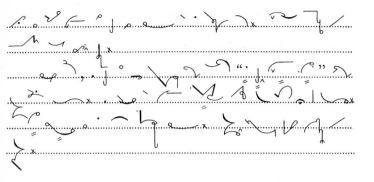

49

Transcribe the following passage

Transcribe the following passage

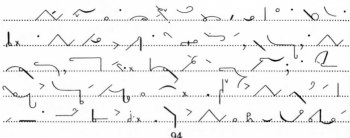

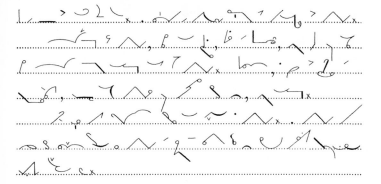

50

Copy the following short forms

incorporated
independent-ly-
   ce

maximum
minimum

indispensable-ly
influential-ly

objective
exchange

intelligence
intelligent-ly

ministry
misfortune

investment
irregular

negligence
notwithstanding

mechanical-ly
messenger

objectionable
passenger

jurisdiction
justification

peculiar-ity
prejudice-d-ial-
   ly

manufacture-d
manufacturer

monstrous
mathematics

Transcribe the following passage

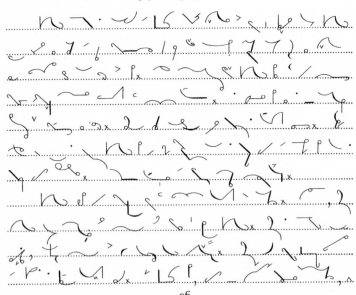

96

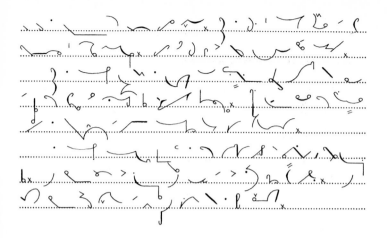

97

51

Transcribe the following passage

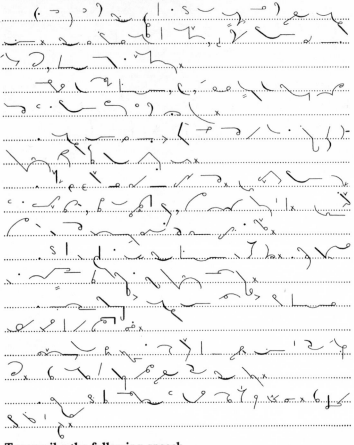

Transcribe the following speech

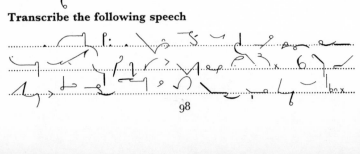

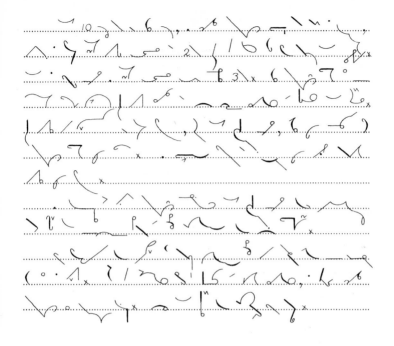

52

Copy the following words containing double strokes

bolder
further

reminder
winters

letter
filter

entering
supplanter

educator
repeater

reflectors
anger

smoulder
inventor

sinker
linger

sector
director

handkerchief
amber

indicator
typewriters

December
pumper

Copy the following intersections

Arts Council
at your earliest
   convenience

Benevolent Society
authority of the
   governor

all your requirements
full insurance cover

previous arrangement
liberal outlook

please do not mention the
   matter
we have received the
   authority

Australian community
new territory

Note: New Zealand

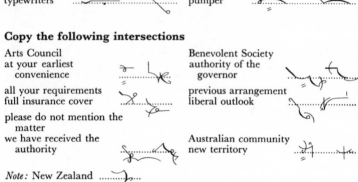

Transcribe the following passage

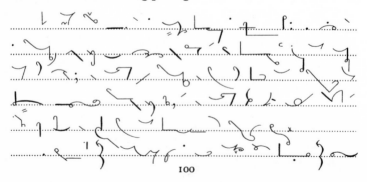

Transcribe the following letter

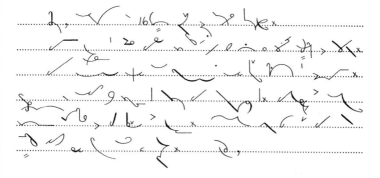

53

Transcribe the following passage

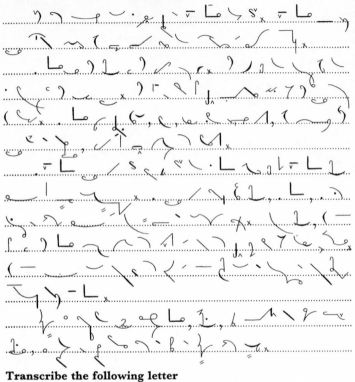

Transcribe the following letter

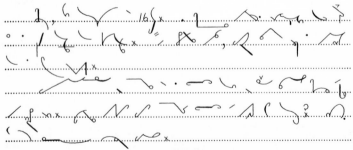

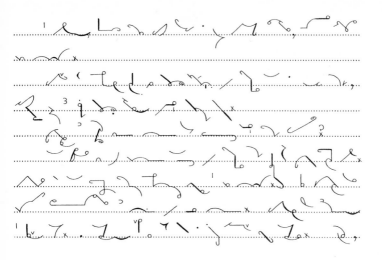

54

Copy the following short forms

perform-ed
performance

subscribe-d
subscription

yard
itself

practicable
preliminary

substantial-ly
suspect-ed

irresponsible-ility
metropolitan

project-ed
proportion-ed

sympathetic
irrespective

obstruction
oneself

prospective
publisher

thankful
unanimous-ly

organizer
proficient-ly-cy

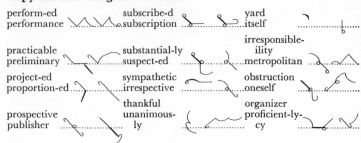

Copy the following words ending in -ns or -nz

dance
one's

announce
France

lanes
vans

experience
occurrence

immense
commence

moans
remains

Transcribe the following passage

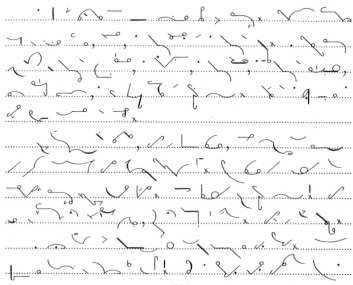

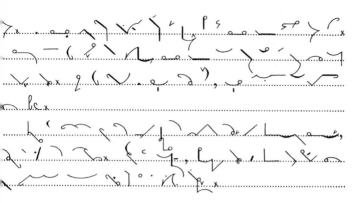

55

Transcribe the following letter

106

Transcribe the following letter

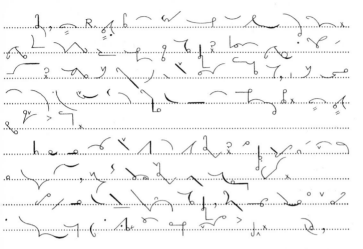

56

Copy the following phrases

will you kindly
will you please

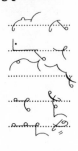

take their place
next month

last month
in five months

six months
seven months' time

six weeks' time
United Nations

North and South
  America
next week the

Chancellor of the
  Exchequer
of considerable

further consideration
as promised

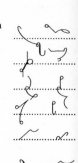

it is suggested
I can assure you

so far as the
set forth

as a rule there is
set off

are not
you are not

they are not
almost certain

in the markets
life assurance policy

Transcribe the following letter

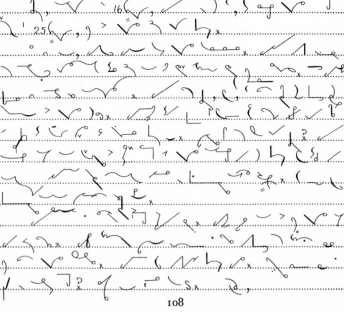

57

Transcribe the following passage

Transcribe the following passage

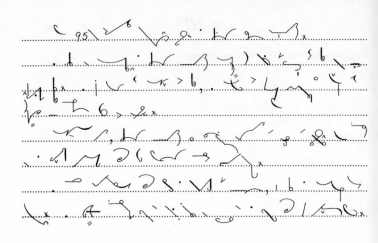

58

Copy the following short forms

questionable-ly
reform-ed

uniform-ity-ly
valuation

irrespective
reproduction

representation
respective

arbitration
distinguish-ed

retrospective
subjection

respectively
selfish-ness

circumstantial
destructive

unprincipled
familiarization

sensible-ly-ility
stranger

generalization
distinguishable

mathematical
irrespectively

howsoever
henceforward

inconsiderate
irrecoverable-ly

cross-
examination
difficulty

Transcribe the following letter

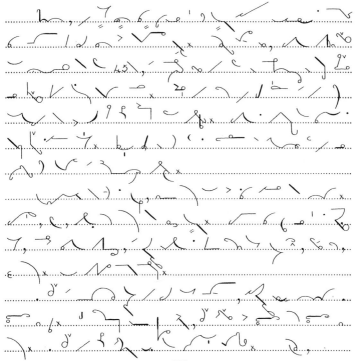

Transcribe the following passage

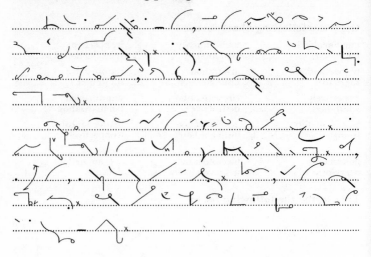

59

Transcribe the following passage

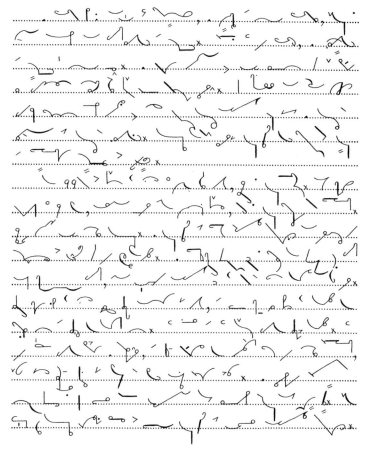

Transcribe the following passage (See note on page 114)

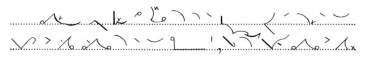

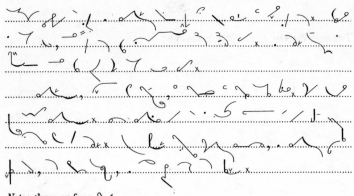

Note: three or four

60

Copy the following sets of distinguishing outlines

hardest
hearty

protect
product

abundant
abandoned

hardiest
heartiest

endless
needless

persecute
prosecute

refer
revere

guarantee
grantee

petrified
putrefied

Copy the following words containing -ful, -fully

peaceful-ly
beautiful-ly

disgraceful
disgracefully

lawful
lawfully

harmful-ly
spiteful-ly

successful
successfully

wakeful
wakefully

Transcribe the following letter

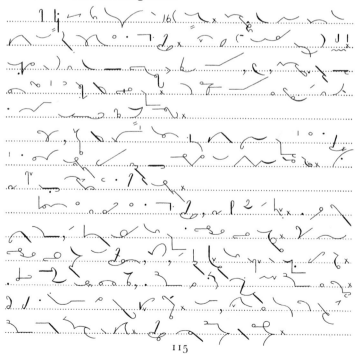

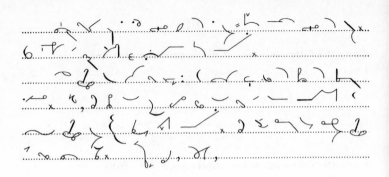